I AM BECOMING!

The God In Me

"A puzzle is only the becoming until it is complete. It is then the results of a whole picture formed from its designated pieces."

By Quintina Alexander

Dedication

Here's an important reminder to our mother. For many are called and few are chosen. You are one of God's strongest daughters. You have seen things so that your family doesn't have to. You have suffered for His name's sake and because of that, I pray that God remembers your name. In my eyes, your good outweighs the bad regardless of your past.

You are phenomenal and inspirational. You taught us the heart of God, and you showed us how to lean on God no matter what. Due to the fact that you are selfless, I hope that you gain everything you desire. Always remember who you are and whose you are. I love you mom.

Contents

Introduction

Have you ever felt lost or confused by the unseen forces shaping your life? Our family certainly did. This book isn't meant to cast the blame on them or to judge anyone's else's path. Instead, it's a story of navigating the complexities of faith and family. Through my experiences, I hope to shed light on the power of spiritual understanding.

For far too long, families have been divided by struggles they don't fully comprehend. I believe that knowledge is the key to unity! As we learn and grow together, we can redirect our struggles towards a more positive force. This isn't about fighting each other or seeking revenge, but rather about channeling our energy through faith and allowing God to be our champion.

Join me on this journey of discovery. Within these pages, you'll find not just our story, but a potential path towards a more harmonious and spiritually fulfilling life for you and your loved ones.

Chapter 1

In The Beginning

May 25,1989, ding dong, special delivery. There I was, born and gifted into the arms of my mother. The most innocent days of a child are the infant era. No worries, no fear, no accountabilities, and no impurities, just pureness at its best. Then you have the babies who are born with a target. The babies who are chosen by God and targeted by Satan.

I was the baby born with a target and surely the enemy awaited my arrival. Satan had a plan set in motion to defeat and kill my purpose. Oh, but God had plans for me to live and prosper. God had chosen me to execute His perfect and good will for my life and His name's sake. He sent me to this earth to use me as His vessel. I did not understand then, but I was surely about to learn alone the way that I was sent not to be conformed to the ways of the world or defeated by them. A child's heart is filled with foolishness, until it is hit with the rod of discipline.

"Foolishness is bound in the heart of a child; but the rod of correction shall drive it far from him" (Proverbs 22:15).

As time went by, I became old enough to distinguish what was good and what was bad. I was at an age of acknowledgement. Therefore, I remember those times when the enemy struck. It was at a time when my mother would leave for work. The moment she closed the door behind her the darkness arose in the middle of the day. It was not just the darkness; it was what was hidden in the darkness.

There I stood facing the wall with my underwear snatched and pulled in between my buttocks. I was instructed to raise and drop my arms up and down, as my hands slapped against my hip structure. I can hear his loud and abnormal breathing.

There I was standing on the enemy's campground, in the eyes of the devil. I was being stripped from my innocence and touched by impurity. I was trembling in the presence of fear. Although I was in its presence, I was not there mentally. As my arms were going up and dropping down hitting my hips and causing my butt to shake, I would close my eyes.

The moment my eyes closed I was on the other side, in my imagination. I was running through a jungle. In the jungle there was a trailer and, in that trailer, lived a man and a child. Every time I walked in the door the child would run to me in excitement and jump in my arms as if I was her savior. The man and I would make this weird eye contact. It was like I knew he was harming that little girl. He had a guilty presence. His guilt and shame were written on the appearance of his face.

I would take the little girl outside behind the trailer. Behind the trailer was a big and empty beach. Just sand and the ocean and a bright sky. There is where this little girl and I played joyfully and in peace until it was time for me to go. She always had this sad look on her face as I was fading away back into reality.

I opened my eyes to the sound of my stepfather's voice. When he was done with me, he would tell me to fix my clothes and tell my sister Neka to come here. Come to find out we were both on the enemy's campground. I only went to this place when I was being violated. There were times when I was not being violated and I tried to close my eyes and go back to the place, but I could not. I know as weird as it may sound and to most it sounds like I had a strong imagination.

In fact, I did. My imagination was my safe place. I did not understand then until I got older in my adulthood that my imagination was God's arms wrapped around me. That was His way of keeping me safe and in His arms. He was my safe place when I was in the danger zone. I grew into the habit of exercising my imagination as a child. No matter what my reality was, my imagination was on the other side of the world. It was beautiful. It was peaceful and there I was happy.

Bedtime was my favorite time. It was my time to go wherever my imagination took me until I fell asleep. And boy, oh boy did it take me to some places. There was always a happy conclusion there. Everything about my imagination was positive and good.

Again, I did not understand what I understand now. The importance of the mind. The mind is what the enemy wants. He wanted in, but with the imagination I had, he could not get in. His distractions were blocked from my mind. I can remember the beginning of the molestation, but I do not remember how far it went past what I have described.

My sister and I both were being molested by him. The difference was our minds. Neka did not have a mindset like mine. Satan's seed had already taken ground in my sister's mind. I learned in my adulthood that your endurance has a lot to do with how your mind is set. If your mind is not set to block Satan's principalities and powers, it will seep within, and you will struggle with sin. That thing will attach itself to your soul. It will not take much of a pull when you try to restrain from his ways. Your sin will become normal for you. Satan is so deceiving. He makes you feel like you are entitled to live that way because of what happened to you and all you have been through. He likes to give out excuses. Yet, that excuse is not going to excuse you into the gates of heaven.

It was Arthur Fletcher who quoted, **"A mind is a terrible thing to waste."** Indeed, it is. There are so many scriptures in the bible that tell us to guard our thoughts. Our minds and hearts are the main lines of connection with God. We must set our minds on Christ, so that our hearts can be filled with desire to fulfill His perfect will.

"Let this mind be in you, which was also in Christ Jesus:" (Philippians 2:5).

"And the peace of God, which surpasses all understanding, shall keep your hearts and minds through Christ Jesus" (Philippians 4:7).

"Trust in the LORD with all thine heart; And lean not unto thine own understanding. In all thy ways acknowledge him, And he shall direct thy paths" (Proverbs 3:5-6).

"And do not be conformed to this world, but be transformed by the renewing of your mind, that you may prove what is that good and acceptable and perfect will of God." (Romans 12:2 NKJV).

Need I go on giving scriptures? There are more than the four, that I gave. It was Helen Keller who quoted, **"The only thing worse than being blind is having sight but no vision."**

The vision is in the mind and the passion is in the heart. The two of them together is the desire to fulfill God's will. My God, I feel a soul being saved. Praise break! Singing Amazing Grace, I once was lost but now I am found. I once was blind but now I see.

Our mother worked long shifts and sometimes she worked two jobs. Neka was left to tend to us. Neka was the oldest. There were six of us, five girls and one boy. My mother was an evangelist, and my stepfather was a preacher and together they served in ministry. My mother was on fire for God. We grew up under the mantle. Mother was a prayer warrior and a demon slayer, yet she missed the demon that was under her nose. The very one that was sent to cause destruction. The one that was touching two of her daughters with its impurities. Her house was under attack, and she had no idea because she was too busy with work and ministry.

It is true an idle mind is the devil's workshop. An idle mind is a mind that has no direction or definiteness of purpose. Your mental doors are open and subjected to any random thought that comes your way. Therefore, it provides a playground for Satan to play on. So, the goal is to keep busy because success operates in active moments and not in idleness. So, remember when you say you are bored that boredom is the devil's delight.

However, keeping busy does not keep him out. In fact, it is an advantage. Remember he is smart he just lacks power if not given. Do not be too busy to step back and see what is going on in your own personal life. Take time to evaluate your well-being, kids, your spouse, and your household. Make sure you cover everything. Do a thorough check into the issue your kids bring to you even if it seems small and irrelevant to you. Check for any leaks in your home.

We know that small leaks can become a big water bill. So do not be so busy caring for the outside, that you do not have time to address what's on the inside. Especially us women. We are the glue to our home, and we are responsible for a lot. We must remain watchful while doing our duties. We have to say prayers that will watch over our families when they are not in our presence. We must wake up at certain hours of the night and war out over our household and family.

Remember who the serpent went for first. It was the woman. So, we must be tough in our position. He sees us as an easy target. It is ok to be comfortable in your home but with a target on your back your comfort is limited. There are and will be times where there is just no time for comfort until God gives you permission to rest. Those are the times we must ask Him to arm us in His strength.

Eventually, what was in the dark would soon be exposed in the light. The light started shining in through the observations of my grandmother. She expected Neka was being violated.
She noticed how every time my stepfather had to make a store run, he only wanted to take Neka. Out of the five girls and one boy you would think it would have been my brother he would have taken with him. You know like the father and son thing.

I Am Becoming

When I was in head start during restroom break, for whatever reason caused my teacher to come in and check on me. I am not sure if I stayed there too long or if it was due to me complaining but it was reported that blood was found in the seat of my panties. This is not a vivid memory to me, but my older cousin mentioned this to me one day when me, her and my mother were discussing how the issue surfaced to the light about molestation. The issue caught the attention of the teacher, and it was reported to social services. One of the ladies that knew about the issue was friends with my aunt and had told her about it. The light had shined into the darkness, and it was time to expose what was hiding in it.

Thank God for the safe place that He kept me in. Some things I would rather not know or remember. I do not ever want to know how far it got from what I already know. It is sickening, and hearing my cousin tell me about the blood in my panties and I was only in head start made me cringe. I know the memories I do have; I was a little older than head start age. So, it is my best assumption that this had to have been going on for quite some time.

This must have caused an uproar on my mother's side of the family. My grandmother had my male cousins to jump on my stepfather. My mother did what she felt was right, she honored her vow to her husband for better or for worse. She sided with him and her decision to stand by her husband caused a fight between her and two of her sisters. This had transpired in my grandmother's trailer. Little did they know, choosing to handle this with physical violence had no effect. They could not beat the demon out of him that way. The attack had been in play, but the destruction was just beginning.

My mother was everyone's favorite aunt. She was the one lady in the neighborhood that gathered the kids in the community for bible study and fed them snacks. She was a kingdom worker, a wife and a mother. Before she became a follower of Christ, I heard she was the life of the party back in the day. She had an identity, and she knew it. She learned her identity the moment she turned her back against the world.

When your back is against the world you are no longer camouflaged. You are no longer the hidden target. You stick out like a sore thumb and your only safe place is in God. You are the one Satan is looking to devour and he will stop at nothing and only the hand of God will avenge you.

You may be strong and in a safe place but remember the company you keep can be an open entrance to the enemy. Sometimes jealousy is a friend. A good friend, too good to recognize. This is one of the many experiences that I had to go through and each time I suffered.

Finally, I learned and took heed. **Shut up and keep them shut out.** This is basically saying that by keeping your mouth closed, you keep others out of your business. You keep them clueless. One thing about it, Satan knows you are aware of him, so he may be in one place while his devils are in another. He stops only at the hand of God. Set limitations on your friends while trusting God to give you friends.

"It is better to trust in the LORD than to put confidence in man" (Psalms 118:8).

While our mother was slaying demons, her husband, the man who vowed to love, honor and protect her, left her back uncovered. She must have felt stripped down to her nakedness. Shame must have barricaded her. Her family knew too much of her personal business to stay in town. It was time to take her family and go.

She had taken us and left town without her husband. My mother did not have a plan. She did not know where we would go but she knew she wanted to be away from all the drama that had transpired. She knew she wanted her marriage to work. Running was her choice of action. We ended up in a shelter in Meridian, Mississippi for a few days and nights.

She then made the decision to come back to Mississippi, but it was not to stay, she came back to get her husband. She packed up our things and picked up her husband and we left Mississippi, leaving behind our home. We lived in a genuinely nice trailer out in the country with my stepfather's family. She gave it all up. She thought it would be easier to just leave and start over rather than to face what was up against her.

Some problems can be left behind, but this problem was beyond a problem. This problem was only the shifting of her storm. Little did she know this storm was sure to follow and her choices were causing it to grow bigger. Satan's plan was at play. We were on the road to wherever. My mother was in survival mode.

We slept in our van from parking lot to parking lot. We were living on the go. We ate sandwiches, chips, cookies, Vienna sausages and potted meat. A lot of nights we went without hot meals and baths. From shelters, to eating at the Salvation Army. Going through all this my mother still tried to continue her walk with God. She and my stepfather were preaching on the side of the road and in parking lots. I can even remember us just randomly attending a tent revival. Shame or not, my mother pushed it all to the side and asked for help from whomever would give it. We ended up in Mobile, Alabama. We attended different churches. We even lived in the back of one of the churches and I do not mean the back parking lot.

Eventually, we settled down in Saraland, Alabama. We moved into some apartments called Queensburgh. It was the project, but it was better than sleeping in a van, at least that is what I thought. It was a two-story apartment with five bedrooms and two full bathrooms. My mother and stepfather found work and we were enrolled in school. Things were falling back into place, yet the storm was still on the radar. Little did mother know she had moved us into a dead zone. Shortly after moving in, some strange things started happening in that apartment.

One of the bedrooms was our playroom. We kept our bikes in storage there. The stranger things around that apartment got, the more danger we were in. One day after we all returned home the bikes had been moved differently than when we left them. Now this was not just something one person was noticing; we were all noticing the strange things. My mother prayed about it. In that apartment my mother continued having bible study with us every night before bed. She was always praying and fasting. Her anointing must have been what aroused those demonic encounters.

The calling on her life was calling out her enemies. It must have started the day she said yes to God. A lot of people did not accept who she was as a Christian. They believed that her walk with Christ was fake. A look of doubt appeared on their faces when she started talking "Christian talk". They did not understand the new lingo. These same individuals chose to judge her new way of life with her previous lifestyle of partying and hanging around the wrong people.

Maybe she was not running, what if she was just following the bible. Jesus did tell His disciples to leave home or town if anyone would not welcome or listen to their words. She had a different perception from her spiritual eye than what others saw on the outside. Or to her, it was a case of false accusation attacking her husband's anointing, rather than how others saw it as her choosing her husband over her kids. He was attacked but not by false accusations.

His attack was in his mind. His actions were not of God. That was the work of Satan.

One day my mother and aunt were downstairs praying or in bible study. My stepfather was gone. My little sisters were in their room playing. Me, Neka, and our brother were upstairs in the playroom playing double Dutch. It was Neka's turn to jump, while we turned the jump ropes, she had started complaining about her head hurting.

She then pointed her finger towards me and said she saw something standing behind me. She said it was something big and black with red eyes. Neka meddled so much I did not believe her I thought she was just trying to scare us. Within a matter of seconds, she started drooling from her mouth and she started talking in this strange voice. Her head fell to the side, and she was struggling to walk straight. She mumbled in a creepy and raspy voice, "Get out my house bitch." Immediately, I went into action running out the room yelling from the top of the staircase, "Ma something is wrong with Neka, she's cussing."

As I am telling my mother what happened, my sister is coming out of the room staggering and loudly repeating "Get out!"

By this time, my mother and aunt are standing at the end of the staircase as Neka starts to come down. Mother yelled for us to go back into the room. She started calling on Jesus, rebuking and speaking in tongues. Neka had been possessed by a demon. I stood in the hallway listening to my mother and aunt war over my sister with that demon. After some time, it left her body, but its presence was still in the apartment. It was to the point where my mother had everyone sleeping downstairs in the living room. She must have had some sleepless nights watching over her family in prayer.

We are kids so of course we were scared. We had never seen anything like this, not even on tv. Mother did not allow us to watch scary movies. She limited the cartoons we watched. We would not even go to the bathroom alone. If one of us had to go upstairs for something, another had to come along with that person.

One night mother was cooking, and this memory is still so vivid. I was standing at the entrance of the kitchen. She had taken a pan of barbecue chicken out of the oven and sat it on the back of the stove top. She went to the other side of the kitchen for something. Suddenly, I saw the pan slide up to the front of the stove top and fall to the floor. My mother turned around. We were both stunned. She started calling on the name of Jesus and rebuking its presence.

Next door lived this lady, and she had a set of twins. If I remember correctly, their names sounded very similar to Neka's real name, which is Tamaneka. Neka and those girls became friends. Our mothers both made contact one day and started talking. The lady told my mother her brother used to live in the apartment we lived in. She explained that he was an old drunk and he was involved with a lady who was also involved with another man that lived in the building across from the building we lived in.

The situation got bad between the two men. They got into an argument that turned deadly. Her brother was stabbed to death in the kitchen of the apartment we lived in. That explained the punctured holes in the top door of the refrigerator. She said ever since his death, no one that moved in that apartment stayed long. She was surprised we stayed as long as we did. It also makes more sense why Neka struggled to walk and was staggering like a drunk when she was possessed.

Seemed like everything about that environment was dark including the people. We dealt with attempted break ins amongst other things. For an example, late on Christmas Eve night Neka and I were cleaning the kitchen spotless. It was late in the midnight hour and we all know that those presents will make a child walk a straight line.

We were finishing up and someone started kicking the back door really hard. The kitchen light was on, so they had to know someone was home. Me and Neka took off running down the hallway and up the stairs yelling at our parents. She was ahead of me, and I went to pull on her shirt trying to keep up and she elbowed me in the nose. I had a bad nosebleed. When they went to check it out there was a footprint left on the door.

Mother no longer wanted to risk our lives living in that apartment. It was time to go. This time she made plans to move. It was not just a get up and go. We moved to another set of apartments. It was not the suburbs, but the environment was a little better.

Once again, mother just wanted a fresh start. Yet the storm seemed to have followed us at every turn. It continued to grow even bigger and darker, as we stood in the eye of it. We returned home one day only to see our home had been broken into. It seemed as if the problems there kept coming back-to-back.

Neka was quite the fighter. She had to be around 11 or 12 years of age when she fought this 18-year-old girl. For some reason, this girl used to pick on Neka. Her name was Monica. Neka was not your typical fighter at her age. One day Neka called her out. What problem could Monica have had with my sister, I do not know, but when I say Neka put a whooping on that girl with an orange, plastic baseball bat. That's exactly what I mean.

The bat was flattened too, so you know the edges on the bat scratched and cut into her skin. I can imagine how that steamy water boiled into her whelps when she got into the shower that night.

More problems occurred and again it was time to go. My mother had met a queer Caucasian man named Curt. Curt had a long ponytail. He lived in a trailer park. He opened up his doors to my mother and her family. And the storm grew darker. Seemed like the darker this storm got the less fight she had to give. She had become weary on her journey.

It was just what Satan wanted. The wearier and faint she became; the stronger Satan's grip became. My mother started sliding back little by little. My mother had started smoking cigarettes and drinking wine coolers. She and her husband were drifting apart. She was so distracted she did not even notice that Neka was venturing out into the world of promiscuity.

Neka started dating this boy who lived in the trailer behind Curtis. He was a little older than her. His name was Mardell. Mardell had a sister, and she too was being promiscuous. Their mom was rarely ever there and when she was it was as if she was not. Her kids were open around her. This boy had Neka's nostrils wide open. I guess she had found an escape in pleasure.

His sister was grooming Neka's appearance. Neka started acting out almost becoming an entirely different person. I hated that boy because I felt as if he was taking my sister away from me. Me and Neka used to always play grown-ups with turtlenecks on our heads pretending it was our long hair. He had gotten in the way of our play time.

Our play time became his time. My sister and I were like two peas in a pod. We did things that siblings would enjoy together. For an example, we used to plan out our double weddings, she scared my bullies away and things of that nature. He did not break our bond but, he was interfering with our relationship. We had lived in some uncomfortable places and this place was the one I hated most.

Meanwhile, the wind was picking up more speed. The storm was not slacking. One thing led to another and once again, social services were back in our lives. The wind had blown them back into our path. Only this time actions were taken. We were in the custody of social services. This must have been the turning point for my mother.

They separated the six of us by twos and placed us into three different foster homes. My grandmother and aunt came to Alabama and so did my stepfather's sisters. They would not release us back into my mother's care. My grandmother was not allowing us to be separated so she stepped in. She sure as well was not allowing his sisters to take any of us.

They released us into my grandmother's custody, and we came back to Mississippi. My grandmother lived in a two-bedroom trailer in Foxworth, Mississippi.

Somehow, my mother did get us back. I say somehow because I do not quite remember how it happened. What I do remember is she was not the same. She was spiraling out of control. She had stopped going to church and started going to clubs. Her altar became men.

She was into party life and hanging out with her nieces. Many nights we were left alone in the dark with no lights while she was dancing under party lights. Neka used to cry with her arms wrapped around us comforting us. Her and my mother's relationship was its own storm.

Neka was consumed with resentment towards our mother. However, it was not just against our mother. Neka did not really get to enjoy her childhood. She took care of us when my mother worked. Helping with us was part of being the oldest sibling, but it became a burden to her. When my mother lost her ability to be our mother. Neka did her best to fill that void. Neka did more than watch us. She cooked for us, combed our hair and got us up while making sure that we were ready for school. She made sure we did our homework, disciplined us when we were disobedient, and she did her best to fill that empty void. Resentment caused hell to rage in her. No one wanted to put up with her attitude.

They didn't have what it took to calm the hell that raged within her. She was counted out. She was labeled as a fast tail gal and a hot head. From their perception all they saw was she wanted to be grown, when in fact she did not. She wanted to be a child, yet she was put in a position to be an adult.

My mother got involved with this man named Jamie. We moved into his trailer with him. He was abusive to her. We did not like him. His actions did not show that he liked us either. He was an alcoholic. My grandmother would come by to check on us and bring us food. She did not care for him either. Neither did she hide it. He acted differently in her presence.

I remember Neka telling me he touched her one night. My mother let Neka sleep in the bed with her on the night it occurred. Neka slept next to my mother, and he was on the other side of my mother. He reached over to my mother and Neka said she felt his hand under her shirt. My mother confronted him about it. They argued back and forth. He claimed it was not intentional and it was dark and that he thought it was my mother he was touching. This must have been the day they fought like a storm coming through the trailer.

It escalated to the outside. I can remember him pulling on her shirt trying to snatch her down from the top step as she braced her leg on the other side of the doorway. I threatened to hit him with the board I was holding. We all helped my mother fight him off. He busted her eye. It was swollen and blackened. One of my male cousins threatened his life if he ever laid another hand on her. He did not have the same energy with my cousin as he did toward my mother.

Somewhere in this era of my life I met my real dad for the first time when I was in the fourth grade. He came and pulled me from class and introduced himself. He gave me five dollars. One of my aunts had a run in with him and told him about our situation. My mother could not seem to get her life back on track.

My daddy showed up in court trying to get me, but my grandmother was not having it. My stepfather's sisters were there in my three younger sisters' defense as before in Alabama. They released us back into the care of my grandmother.

We thought my grandmother was mean. She was of age and just set in her ways. Her ways were not ours or what we were used to. And because of that we thought she was mean. There were orders under her roof, and we had to follow them.

She trained us up with routines, which helped build structure to our daily life. Every morning, we got out of bed, we had to make them up before even coming out of the room, brush our teeth, wash our face, and get dressed for school. On the weekend, we continued that same routine. We put on play clothes.

She cooked us a full breakfast every weekend and after we ate, she would say hit the yard. She had a big yard too. "Hit the yard," meant, "go outside to play." There was no playing in her house. We sat on the floor and ate on a sheet, which was called a piece. When she said get that piece, we knew it was time to eat. She cooked dinner every day of the week. She was not the fast-food type, and we ate what she cooked.

There was no such thing as a picky eater under her roof. She was not big on feeding us junk food. Fruit, cheese puffs or Doritos were our snacks. Oh, and saltine crackers! Although she kept several cases of sodas, they were not for us. Water and juice were our beverages.

When she had company, we knew to go outside unless it was raining and even then, we had better not be caught looking into their mouthes during conversation. She did not play about kids sitting around grown-ups while they talked. When we came from outside, we sat on the floor until we got our baths. She would already start preparing the water for our baths. She did not have hot water, so she had to boil water for our baths and to wash dishes.

There was no walking on her floors all night either and no sleeping all day. Every Saturday, we had to get our school clothes out for the entire week. They had to be ironed and hung. She only had a washer machine. She washed our clothes, and we pinned them on the clothesline. When something was out of order and she asked who did it and everyone hollered, "Not me", we all got whooped for it. So yes, her ways were not the ways we were used to. Her house was in order because she lived by order. If no one else had what it took to make Neka bow down, Mury J. Alexander sure did.

I mean do not get me wrong she spared the rod for all of us. Neka caught the ugly end of the stick though, but it was spared from love. The inner demons raging in her was something to wrestle with. Neka's attitude and behavior was serious. Pure and genuine love is what Neka needed. She was pouring her love into us, and no one was pouring it back into her.

All the while, my grandmother was battling lung cancer and had been for some time. We just did not know. I mean she always went to doctor appointments, but we did not know it was for that reason. One day she came home from the doctor's and called Neka into the room. Then I heard Neka crying.

She later told me what was going on with our grandmother and why she wore turbans. The chemo procedures had taken her hair out. She had some pretty hair. It was solid gray and she kept it parted down the middle and in two braids.

Now this was the news that worried Neka. She said to me, "If something happens to maw maw, it is over for us. No one is going to love us enough to keep all of us together and under one roof." All of us were attentive to my grandmother but, Neka was the most attentive one toward her. The sicker she got the more Neka pulled closer to her. We sat under the shade tree plenty of days praying together for our mother. Hoping she would just pull up. We wanted her to get her life together and do what was necessary to get us back. We went for extended periods without hearing from her.

With each instance, I became more distant. She would call from time to time. After she and maw maw talked, maw maw would pass the phone to one of us and we would all be rushing each other off the phone so the next could talk. She told us the same thing every time, "Mommy's getting herself together" or "I've got an apartment." I promise I am going to get y'all back." My hopes used to jump for joy when I would hear her say that until one day it no longer did.

She would randomly show up every so often with some man, but it was not to get us. Her lies would stretch from one end to the next. She was out in the world with no cover. My mother was too overwhelmed to fight back. Satan had her right where he wanted her. Chained down into his wilderness.

He had taken her stand and weakened her knees. She was no longer standing in faith and kneeling to God. Her identity was stolen. Fear backed her up into a corner and dared her to move. Satan had her chained down with drug addiction and alcohol. He had a stronghold on her and gave her whatever kept her weak.

The chemo treatments left my grandmother drained for some days. She had good days and she had bad days. Yet, she did not let it stop her from tending to our needs. She still stood over the stove and made full course meals for us. She even managed to continue starting up the washing machine. My aunts and cousins helped. We moved to a bigger trailer with more space and rooms out in Tylertown, Mississippi.

My grandmother was the real MVP. She left the comfort of her life just to make our life more comfortable. My grandmother was set. Her trailer was paid for and so was her car. She had a light blue box Pontiac. We never lived without lights and water. She did not have to do that, but she sacrificed. And never did she throw it in our faces.

I can remember her smiling the day we moved in. We were unpacking and putting canned goods into the cabinets.

The only thing that changed was her address, her rules remained the same. We knew what to do without having to be told. On the days she had to go to the doctor, she would drop us off back at her trailer in Foxworth, Mississippi. She would bring the laundry she washed for us to pin it on the clothesline. We did not have one put up in the new trailer. Plus, she was not comfortable leaving us alone in an unfamiliar environment.

One time when she dropped us off in Foxworth, my mother came out of hiding and scared us after my grandmother and cousin left. We were excited to see her. She had been sneaking and living in my grandmother's trailer but she was not alone. Hiding under one of the beds was my stepfather. My excitement faded. She made us promise not to tell my grandmother or anyone else about their being there.

I was in a daze on the ride home. Looking out the window from the backseat and thinking why she was back with him. How could she not hold him accountable? I blamed him. I was angry and bothered. Later that night I disclosed the information. I told my cousin, and she told my grandmother. My siblings were mad at me for telling but I did not care. I did it out of spite against my stepfather. Although I missed my mother and was glad to see her, I was angry with her. It had been a minute since we had seen her.

We did not know her whereabouts. She had not been in contact with us. We were waiting for her to come through on her promises to us but instead she was still honoring her promises to him. For better or for worse. It was most definitely for the worse, living in her mother's trailer with him and without consent. Her mother was sick and was not getting any better. We needed her. Did she not care?

As children, we had no true understanding. We understood only from our emotions and what we heard and what was told to us. To hear someone say to my mother, "You chose a man over your children," and seeing her actions, we believed it. It caused some ill feelings towards her in all of us, especially Neka. The resentment towards my mother consumed all of us eventually. I blamed my stepfather. I hated him and it was all because I did not understand spiritual battles and the power of demonic force.

Satan's grip on her was tight. He gave her the desires of her flesh not her heart. Satan does not give us the desires of our hearts. Our heart is made to love, and love is not in Satan.

If it had not been for my walk with Christ, continuing to love on my mother would have been a challenge to say the least. Thank God for spiritual eyes and ears. She wanted to get her life together. It was what her heart desired, and Satan was not giving into her heart. He was playing against it. My mother had a family. Not just any family but a family under the mantle. She had a Joshua 24:15 family.

"And if it seem evil unto you to serve the LORD, choose you this day whom ye will serve; whether the gods which your fathers served that were on the other side of the flood, or the gods of the Amorites, in whose land ye dwell: but as for me and my house, we will serve the LORD" (Joshua 24:15).

My grandmother's health had taken a turn for the worse. My grandmother was omitted into the hospital. She went into a coma. We were under my cousin's supervision. Our time living under one roof was ending. Neka grew wearier. She feared the day was to come. She encouraged us to pray together as always. My mother trained us in prayer. That was something we always did, and Neka made sure of that.

The day my grandmother had awoken from the coma, we went to visit her. She did not wake up the same. It was as if her mind had been reset to the mind of a baby. She did not talk with words anymore. She did not recognize anyone.

However, she did jump into excitement when Neka walked into the room second behind my cousin. She jumped like how a baby reacts when they see their mother. She recognized Neka or that was God giving Neka a sign that she was special.

The purpose of that sign was to be a memory to serve as a reminder when the enemy made her feel she was not. I know it sounds crazy for me to explain it in this way, but this was one of the memories my sister was sure to carry in the front of her mind. God is the seer over our lives. He knows our future and He know what lies ahead of us in the light and what awaits us in the dark. He not only instructs us, but He equips us for the journey. Even memories have purpose.

My mother was there at the hospital when we walked into the room. We were happy to see her. Yet again, it had been a while. After a brief time, she was getting ready to go. We were sent out into the waiting room. There was a man sitting and Neka asked him if he was there for my mother, and he answered yes. She told him we were her kids. Little did anyone know Neka was contemplating her feelings.

She felt there was no way my mother was about to choose a man over us that day. Anger was wailing into a rage. Her adrenaline was rushing. She sat in that room waiting, trying to hold herself from an outburst.

My mother walked in, and we followed her and the man out to the elevators. By the time my mother got ready to lift her second foot into the elevator, Neka snatched her back. The rage within was now on the outside. Her and my mother were fighting on the 5th floor of the hospital. My cousins ran to break it up. They fell and Neka was on top of my mother bear hugging her so tight. The hug came from a place of pain. She was hurting. We all were but her pain was more intense. My mother stayed. She did not leave.

Now I cannot remember if we had made another visit after this day or if this occurred all in the same day as the fight, but my mother attempted to kidnap us from the hospital. The same man from the waiting room was waiting for us in a van out under the parking garage of the hospital.

I do not know what her purpose was for trying to pull such a thing, but Neka was not allowing it. Although we all wanted to be with our mother (including Neka), Neka was not in agreement with her plan. My mother was demanding us one way and Neka was demanding us the other way. We followed Neka's way.

We did not leave with her. Neka was the only one that had the courage to stand up to her. Neka courage may have saved us from another encounter of molestation or worse. Neka had the gift of seeing in the spiritual realm. She was also a prophetic dreamer.

The time had come. What Neka had feared happened. My grandmother was no longer able to care for us. She needed to be cared for. It was just as she said, no one would love us enough to make the sacrifice my grandmother made for us. We were separated. I was sent to live with my daddy and his family. I was eleven years old when I moved in with them. My three younger sisters went to live with their aunties. Neka and my brother lived with my mother's sister. Not too long after our separation, my grandmother died. And just like that, what once was whole was now broken, shattered into a million pieces. Pieces that took years on years to mend.

Chapter 2

In The Middle of a War

We were used to moving around, so I should have been used to adjusting. The problem was I had never had to adjust without my siblings. Adjusting never felt so uncomfortable and unbearable as it did when I moved in with my daddy and his family. I did not know them. They did not know me. Eventually, I adjusted to the environment, but my problem with adjusting was by far the issue.

This was an internal issue which later kept me shut in my room. Now when I first moved in with them, I did not have a room. I slept on the couch. So, I did not have a personal space to hide other than in my imagination. That was my safe place no matter where I was. I was enrolled back into the school I started in. The good thing about that was I got to see Neka.

My brother was sent to live with one of our cousins and his wife. He attended school elsewhere and so did my three younger sisters.

We had authorized visits set up. They were limited. I looked forward to those visits. We all did. The dreadful part of those visits was the ending. If I remember correctly, they only gave us two hours together. After so long the visits stopped. We saw each other randomly just by being in the same place. When social services stopped the visits no one took the initiative to keep it going.

The trailer I lived in with my daddy's family had burned down. I went and lived with my old art teacher whom I randomly just started calling my god mama until they got everything back situated. They later got a new trailer and for the first time I had my very own room. I was glad about it, but I would have rather shared this room with all my siblings.

Although I did not like where I was, I had a steady home. Unlikely, Neka and my brother bounced around amongst family, group homes and foster homes. They could not adjust either. They did not want to live in most of those homes. Some of the foster parents had hearts that were not in the right place. It was more beneficial than purpose.

Once they got them, they learned they did not want to keep them for the long run. I guess they can say they tried but they could not handle their attitudes. These people grew weary of wrestling with the resentment that filled Neka and my brother. So, they did what they thought was best for themselves and gave them back to the system. That just made matters worse.

My poor brother. He was the only boy. And because we were not together, he could not protect his sisters. He had never met his real daddy or any of the family from that side. My younger sisters ended up living with my stepfather and his new wife.

Many issues come from resentment. It is a challenging wall to tear down. It is not easy dealing with a person who shows bitterness and disappointment. In fact, it is much easier to walk away from or give up on than to wrestle with it. You cannot fight fire with fire. It takes a heart filled with the love of God, and a powerful word. A lot of praying, teaching and preaching. It requires scripture, consistency, listening and encouragement. It takes testimonies, interceding on that person's behalf. It takes fasting, an anointing and not a degree. This is kingdom work.

Most of the time the person dealing with resentment is mad with God. Some people really do not know how God's love works because they look for a feeling. They do not understand it. So, when they encounter someone who is filled with it, they do not recognize it. **"If God loved me, why would He allow me to suffer like this?"** This is how it feels. This is how Satan wants them to feel.

Again, Neka and I were like two peas in a pod in our childhood. We managed to keep our bond even after they separated from us. No matter where they moved her, she called and wrote me letters. She had lived amongst my mother's family and her real daddy's family. Foster homes and group homes. Eventually, even the system had grown weary of Neka. They were tired of finding her a home because of her behavior.

She was out of the system's hand at this time. She was 16 and considered grown. She even asked the judge if she could take custody of us, but of course they would not favor that. Yet, they thought it was okay for her to provide for herself. The system failed her. They gave up on her. She encountered more sexual abuse while she was in the system. She stood up against the people who thought they could mistreat her because of her circumstances. Her behavior had spiraled out of control.

They could not trust her, and she would not trust them. The infliction of pain on her was much too overwhelming. She mourned for my mother, and my grandmother. She could not get my grandmother back, so she went after my mother. In this era of time, my mother was stoned cold gone off drugs. She was trapped in a hard place to escape, and Satan made sure of that.

Even in the state of her drug addict lifestyle Neka moved in with her. It was not my mother's place. She was living with an older man. She and Neka slept in the same room. They shared conversations about my mother getting herself cleaned and getting their own place.

Neka saw how desperate my mother was to feed her addiction. My mother was working as a housekeeper at this old and raggedy motel. It was a cheap motel.

Some days Neka walked with my mother to work. The distance from where they lived, and the motel was quite a bit of distance to walk.

Neka had watched my mother clean several rooms only for them to pay her six or seven dollars and not per room. This must have been another level of pain for her to have to watch my mother be strung out on drugs.

She witnessed an era of my mother's life we did not. I mean we saw her, but Neka lived with her. The desperate desire for drugs led my mother to stealing from Neka and that led to them fighting. Neka worked by herself. She had to make a living for herself, but that was not going to happen with my mother's condition. She eventually left. The boy Neka was dating was like her knight in shining armor. He was a significant help to her. He was there with her through some rough stages in her life and he loved her.

When she left my mother, she moved in with my aunt. Her and my aunt's daughters had their share of encounters. That later ended. She had gotten involved with another boy. This was one of the most toxic relationships Neka had. The boy was very abusive. However, she put her dukes up and fought back. And one thing about Neka, she was leaving a mark for remembrance.

She moved in with one of our male cousins and his family. My brother was living there too. He took care of them. She saw him serve my mother drugs once, who is his aunt. She could not believe he was serving his aunt. She confronted him but he had the dope boy mentality. That was how he made his living for his family.

Neka felt like that was a kick in the face. She did not understand how he could watch her kids mourn for her and yet serve her the same drugs that kept her down. He did not see it that way. He, himself, was blinded by money. He was not to blame. He was just a pawn to Satan's plan against my mother.

"Satan does not care who he uses to get who he wants. He uses whoever is an opportunity for him."

Meanwhile, I spent a lot of my time isolated in my room and somewhere in my head. Imagination time worked for me. It not only kept me safe but happy. I knew from my childhood I was different when I waited for God to send two of His angels down to get me and take me to Him. Being different felt good to me. I did not fit in, and I was okay with that.

"However, I had opposition on both sides, out and in. The opposition I was facing on the outside inflicted an internal opposition. I was under attack from both sides. The outside enemy had an enemy on the inside. Yet, I was facing the one on the outside not recognizing the one on the inside."

" For we wrestle not against flesh and blood, but against principalities, against powers, against the rulers of the darkness of this world, against spiritual wickedness in high places" (Ephesians 6:12).

Art was another escape for me. I loved to draw. I had a burning desire to become a fashion designer and a model. I drew out my designs. I named every piece I drew. This girl from around the way wanted an unusual look for her senior prom. Her idea was to wear pants not a dress. Everyone knew I had a passion for drawing and designing. She described the look she wanted. I designed a female version tuxedo, and I named it the diamond laced tuxedo.

I was highly creative with the details of the tuxedo. When I presented it to her, she was incredibly pleased. Of course, I did not know how to sew but we knew a lady from the church we attended who made a living from making clothes. Ms. L. Jackson. She was so skilled in sewing. She made my design just as it was on the paper. She did not have a sewing pattern to go by.

She went off the drawing and the details I wrote explaining the parts of the suit. It was all white. If I am not mistaken, she had a white cane stick to go alone with her tuxedo. She was too clean for a date. A male would not have stood the chance standing next to her in his tuxedo. She was stunning. She won best attire. I was in 7th or 8th grade when I designed it.

I made a portfolio of my designs and mailed them off to Oprah Winfrey and Tyra Banks studio. I was a fan of Tyra's talk show and America's Top Model. I looked up Oprah's and Tyra's studio address on the internet. My hopes were set high on hearing a response one day. I emailed their websites with my story and about my designs. I had a peculiar ambition.

When I was not shut off in my room, I was outside in the backyard listening to music. I wanted to be a singer and write music too. I even started a group with this girl. We called ourselves Harmonee.

Even though years had passed I still wanted my mother. I still cried for her. My daddy allowed me to go stay weekends at my aunt when my sister and brother lived there. Some of those times I got to see my mother. She was still promising to get herself clean. Drugs had her looking so bad. She had really lost herself and her appearance. Although I missed her, I had some ill feelings towards her too.

My stepmom and I did not have a mother and daughter bond. We had a basic relationship. I never called her mom. I wanted to in the beginning because I was trying to blend in and I wanted acceptance. However, my stepsister made it truly clear to stick to calling her by her name because that was her mom. I did not want her mother anyway. I wanted my own mother. I did not even want to be there. I cried many nights wishing things had been different. I had a wall of resentment. I was alone in what I felt. No one in that household understood me, at least that is how I felt. One of my stepbrothers and I were cool.

I silenced my emotions through creativity. Me and my stepsister had our share of difficulties. It was a bittersweet kind of thing. When we were good, we were good. When we argued, we did not talk to each other for weeks and it seemed like every time got longer.

She was the one that kept my hair permed. When we argued we had absolutely nothing to do with each other. This is how I started perming my own hair. I had to show her I did not need her. Her sarcasm was a bit much and it became pessimistic. So, we always bumped heads. I had a defensive attitude. Once I learned how to stand up for myself, I did not back down.

My daddy and I did not share a bond either. He was always gone somewhere. I needed to be nurtured. He did not know how to connect with me. I was angry with him. I had my reasons. He may have stood up for me in the courtroom, but he did not stand for me when I needed him most. He made it seem like I was always wrong when I went to him about something. If only he had paid more attention and opened up the lines of communication with me.

I saw how my stepmom showed favoritism when it came to her daughter. And I was not the only one. Because of this I never made a real connection with my stepmom. In fact, I did not like her for this reason. I did not feel like she liked me either. I never accepted her as my mother figure. I just saw her as my daddy's wife. Do not get me wrong, she was not a monster. She just did not fill that void for me. I did not like how she favored her daughter and not me.

I was so jealous. I desired to share a mother and daughter bond with her but I did not get that. I wanted to share a father and daughter bond with him but I did not get that either. I longed for attention. This type of conflict created internal issues within me. Therefore, I suffered from abandonment and rejection issues.

I wanted to be somewhere I felt accepted. I did not want to be an outcast anymore. I was an outcast even when I lived with my mother. She treated me differently. It was not just some made up thought, it was true. My aunts and cousins even took notice of it. Yet I still loved and wanted her. She had her reasons. I confronted my mother when I became an adult and she finally admitted some things to me. I asked her why she treated me like she hated me.

Her response was that she was jealous of me because I took her sister. She explained after she had me, my aunt had taken an attachment to me, and I got in the way of her and her sister's bond. She and my aunt had a bond like me and Neka. My mother was the baby out of four girls.

My aunt helped look after my mother. She helped with raising her. This sounded all too familiar. I understood that feeling all too well. That was how I felt towards the boy Neka got involved with in Alabama when we were kids. My mother carried this hate towards me all the way into my adulthood.

On the contrary, my living circumstances at my daddy's house were good! I did not lack in my physical well-being, and I never starved. I had clothes on my back, and I had a stable home. Yet, that did not fix my internal conflicts. In fact, my internal opposition grew in rage even more. I did not know my vision was not 20/20. I was seeing the way my opposer wanted me to see.

I cried out to God. I had a lot of whys that needed to be answered. Why did I have to be an outcast? Why did He allow this to happen to me and my family? Why was me and my sister molested? Why was I different? Why couldn't I have my mother?

Being different was cool at first, but then I got tired at one point of being different. My internal opposer became exceedingly furious for acceptance. It made me want attention. It was raging. I wanted to be in a place where I felt accepted. Some place where I wouldn't feel like an outcast. I grew weary, and then this. I had decided to take matters into my own hands and I jumped from a moving car. I opened the car door and threw myself out of the moving car. My daddy was driving. I really did a number on my body and skinned myself up from that jump. This was in 2005 after Hurricane Katrina hit.

There was no water and no electricity. Walmart had just opened back up and was only letting so many people in. One of my step cousins ridiculed me for jumping out of that car. Yet the matter was serious, but I lived. She started calling me old highway 44 skyscrapers.

I did not take offense to it. In fact, we still laugh about it now as we are still friends. When she asked me what I was thinking, I told her death. Yet I lived, bandaged up like a mummy, but I lived. I will never forget, and she will not let me. We were walking in Walmart and there I was limping and covered in gauze, an old lady was like, "oh my gosh baby, did you get hit by the hurricane?" We must have laughed so hard.

"Being different comes with a heavy burden. I did not understand how to carry it. I did not know I needed to protect it. I did not know that the opposition on the outside and inside was attacking what God made special about me. I did not know then what I know now."

I was determined to leave my daddy's house. I anticipated turning eighteen. I had an ambitious dream. I was going to live out my desires and become a big-time designer and a supermodel. My plans were to leave my daddy's house the day of my eighteenth birthday. Not the next day, not a minute over. My plans were made, and nothing was going to stop me.

Chapter 3

Happy 18th Birthday

My hand was turning the doorknob of the front door on May 25th, 2007. The time had come for me to exit that life and chase after my dream. I remember my daddy saying to me he had custody over me until I turned nineteen. I laughed because I had already spoken to someone about that matter, and she assured me eighteen was the age I could leave if I wanted to. And I wanted to. The whole time my daddy feared the choice I was making.

"Because I was blinded by an internal opponent, I overlooked what mattered. My daddy and stepmom did their part. They loved me, I just could not see it. Love is not a feeling. They provided a delightful home for me. It was nothing they could have done more to fix me. It was a problem for me to fix. And leaving their house was the best move I could have made because I found the solution in my path."

My plan sounded so easy to execute. I wanted so badly to be in a place where I felt accepted. I wanted to fit in. And there I was out in the world on my own. Free to be.

I moved in with my stepmom's sister and from there I would sleep from pillar to post. Nights here, days there. On the go. A little while there, a little while here.

I was pregnant with my first child at age eighteen while still sleeping from pillar to post. I moved back in with my stepmom's sister right before I was due to give birth. After a little while I was back on the go. Still trying to find my place in this world, I had experienced one encounter after another. I started living with my child's grandparents. And then I met the minister.

In December 2008 I took my baby to take some Christmas photos at Sears. He was four months old. The photographer was a lady that was sweet and truly kind. Her presence was warm and welcoming. My baby was jolly in her presence. He was smiling big and beautiful at every snap. I asked her if she had any kids and she said no. The conversation went on from there.

She began testifying to me, right there in that photo room with no door. The lady was a young minister, who was so enthused when she talked about God. She invited me to go to church with her and gave me her number. I left that photo room feeling different than when I came in.

I did not call her right away because I was not ready to go to church. In fact, I did not call her at all. Two months later February 13, 2009, I got in trouble with the law. I was caught shoplifting and charged with a felony. I will never forget how I felt when that man touched my shoulder right before I was about to walk out of that store and told me I was too pretty for that. I was not by myself. Now, I have had my share of sitting in the back of a police car and mugshots taken in my school days, but this was not that.

I was not scared back then because I knew that they wouldn't keep me as a minor. Again, this was not that. I was scared and I was in trouble. Most of all I was worried about my baby. He was not with me when I got caught. I left him with his grandmother. I left him to do such stupid things like committing a crime. A crime that carries a five-year sentence. You know how the saying goes, "People never seem to find God until they go to jail."

Well, that person was me. They had a church session in that jail house, and I attended. I must have given my life to God without delay. I was scared straight. I had to stay a day and a half. Almost two because it was nighttime when I was released. That is all it took to break me from that nonsense. Thank God for change and for the good people who came and bonded me out.

The next day after my release, I woke up with an urge to go to church, but I did not have a church home. I remembered the minister who photographed my son's Christmas pictures. However, the phone I had her number in was left at the jailhouse. I was too scared to go back and get it. The urge grew stronger. My child's uncle had a female friend that was visiting him. When she was getting ready to leave, she mentioned something about church. I told her that I wanted to attend as well and the next day she came to pick me up.

We walked into the church during praise and worship service. There were a lot of people there. Shortly after taking my seat, I stood up to see the lady that was singing because she was raising the roof! Meaning, that she had the vocal skills of an Angel. To my surprise, I was looking at the minister who took my baby's photos. She was the lady singing "The Devil's Off Of Me". This must have been my sign from God that I was meant to be there. I left that service feeling revived. I left with a fire shut up in my bones! I left wanting to return. The church is named Dominion and Power and I joined after a few visits.

"God prepares the way for us. He knows who to set in your path and when. He sets the place and time."

"To everything there is a season, and a time for every purpose under heaven" (Ecclesiastes 3:1).

It was not by coincidence nor was it by luck. Simply put, it was Gods will for me to walk in and for me to meet that minister. That urge was from God. It was His will for me to go to church with that lady. The very church I was invited to was by minister Keisha who is now known as Psalmist Keisha Brown Cooley. My friend. My inspiration. My sister.

It was God's will to bring me in connection with my birthplace and my spiritual family. Keisha had taken me under her wing. We had prayer sessions and bible studies together. We fasted together and we went to church. She was the first friend that I did this with. That is what I was raised doing when I lived with my mother.

Even though I never stopped praying, I was not picking up the bible. My mother had always read it and taught it to me. No one did that at my daddy's house. I went to church but only because I was made to go. I was not into what was being preached, I was on my phone and thinking about some nappy head boy. Keisha helped teach me how to study the bible. She was the first friend I had lived with that walked in the opposite direction of the world. I witnessed her personal lifestyle. She was not a Christian on Sunday and a stripper by night.

When I first started going to Dominion and Power, my baby and I would attend faithfully. This was the first church I had ever attended that had my ears opened. I was not just listening but, I was paying close attention to the words. I now understand why I had to come in connection with my birthplace. I needed to be under an anointing that matched the anointing on my life.

I could not have grown anywhere else. I needed shaping. I needed to be molded. I needed to be healed. I needed to be covered. I needed to understand my kind of anointing.
I started discovering my identity in Christ. One of the greatest things my mother could have ever done for me, and my siblings was train

us up in prayer and teach us about God. She was not there to warn me about the things in the wilderness, but she taught me the path.

The path that will not let me depart from it no matter how many devils have tried to pull me off. I have been pulled into some of the wrong places. Some places I should not have been, but I kept coming back to the same path. Because of this, I lived in a fruitless cycle.

"Train up a child in the way he should go: And when he is old, he will not depart from it" (Proverbs 22:6).

Although I had started going to church, I still had internal and external opposition. But this time was different because I was under a spiritual covering with better examples. I was no longer naked. I was still on my rollercoaster from one place to another. One encounter after another. Mishaps after mishaps. One Sunday Apostle Cord prophesied a car in my life. He told me he saw me getting a car. He even told me the color of the car I was going to get and so on. At that time, I did not have a vehicle, nor did I have a stable home.

It was not long after he gave me that prophecy, I had bought my first car. A little white Honda Accord. It was in the year 2010. Boy was that car my altar. I spent some nights and days crying in that car and banging my head against that steering wheel trying to figure it all out.

I got tired of living with people. I got tired of people period. Came with too many problems. I started sleeping in my car. I did not take my son through this with me. I would take him to his grandmother. This was not the plan I had when I left my daddy's house. I had a pretty good plan for my life. With that being said, where did all of this ugliness come from? Why was this tedious path chosen for my life?

I did a little local modeling and photoshoots. I even auditioned for America's Next Top Model after the second attempt. I missed my chance in 2011 when I did not take the first opportunity for the weakest reason. The Elect Lady was not pleased with me, and neither was my photographer because we both put our hearts and time into building my portfolio. This is the year I moved into my first apartment.

The day of the audition I was in my apartment wrestling with myself. I wanted to attend the audition, and I was set to go but then I started wrestling with doubt. So many negative thoughts came against me and like an egg, I cracked. I laid in that bed feeling sorrowful for myself and crying like a pitiful fool. I was an emotional wreck.

My life was in a downward spiral. My decision to leave my daddy's house at the age of eighteen was beating me down. I kid you not, but I did not move back. And it is not a decision I have ever regretted. Not even when I was sleeping in my car.

I have regretted some things but, that was not one of them. That decision brought me to a house that helped birth my anointing. If I had not found my identity in Christ, I would not have been able to tell you my story with spiritual understanding and wisdom. I would not have ever known that my internal opponent was me. I was the little girl in that trailer from my imagination.

Chapter 4

The Seed of Discord

"A worthless person, a wicked man, walks with a perverse mouth; He winks with his eyes, He shuffles his feet, He points with his fingers; Perversity is in his heart, He devises evil continually, He sows discord" (Proverbs 6:12-14 NKJV).

"Sowers of discord sow the seeds of bitterness, anger, distrust, and hatred into the ground of other people's hearts. These actions do not come from the spirit of God but are birth from hell from the deceiver the devil. Seeds of discord manifests the works of the flesh."

My stepfather used to say to me, "I don't know what happened to you, you used to be your momma's good child?" I never understood what he meant by that because I was not a bad child, so why was he saying that to me? This came right from the man's mouth that was molesting me. The man that was being controlled by one of the devils that was on my back. That was the seed of discord.

He said it a few times. I started seeking the "why" in his negative opinion about me. This really bothered me. What exactly did he mean by that statement? His remark became imbedded within my brain. I leaned into my own understanding for my answer. I would say to myself, "I used to be good? Good until he touched me? Good until our family was disrupted because of him? Good until he got exposed?" I mean what else could it be? My understanding made me grow angry and furious. This is what the seed of discord was meant to do. It's designed to bring out the anger in you. You become the accuser. You find everyone to blame for your downfalls but yourself. You become needy. Needy for approval, attention and even acceptance. All these things became me. In addition to that, I was experiencing separation anxiety as well. It made me my own opponent. That seed has caused so many problems in my life.

Instead of valuing the truth, I valued the negative opinions of others when it pertained to my identity. That one seed Satan had sown in me from that seed was going up against what God said about me. That joy and peace I had in my imagination had been stolen. When someone told me the truth about me, something that I needed to hear I could not handle it and I argued with them. I went against it. Yet someone said something I wanted to hear, the very something that pleased my internal opposition I accepted. This was a deception at work.

I accepted the lies. I accepted what was easy. I accepted the very things that were hindering me from becoming. I had someone tell me before that it was easier to lie to me than to tell me the truth. Because I argued the truth and the lies, I accepted.

Not only was I assaulted by his hands, but I was insulted by his remark. Satan was using him on the outside of me, He was working to get inside from the outside. Now I understand why God kept me safe in my head, because that is where my joy and my peace resides.

Satan does not want your money or your life. That's just what he uses to distract you. He is a master manipulator. He wants your head. If he attacks the head, the body is spiritually dead. And when you are spiritually dead, what are the odds of your destiny? You cannot live out God's will for your life.

There I was trying to fix myself through the eyes of others, rather than be who I am through the eyes of God. What my stepdad had said to me had gotten into my head and conceived an internal misconception. This caused my thinking to be faulty. And if my thinking was faulty, so was my view.

The seed of discord he sowed in me had taken root in the little girl causing her to open her eyes and see the abandonment, the child neglect and the molestation. And within her it grew a resentful wall. I began to view my life the same way Eve started seeing life once she ate from the tree of good and bad. I saw my nakedness. I no longer saw the little girl at peace and joyfully playing in my head. She saw everything about herself that Satan said she was. Ugly, bald head, skinny and long bodied. And that's not it because I also saw myself as the girl with the funny stance, a monkey, lizard, Olive from Popeye, and even a motherless child. I had become the little sad girl standing on the other side of the mirror. The word of God says that we wrestle not against flesh and blood but against principalities.

"For we do not wrestle against flesh and blood, but against principalities, against power, against the rulers of darkness of this age, against spiritual hosts of wickedness in the heavenly places" **(Ephesians 6:12 NKJV).**

If it had not been for the Lord who was on my side. I would still be on the wrong side of the mirror seeking to be nurtured from the wrong sources. It was not me who needed to be nurtured, it was my spirit and indeed my anointing. Yet I would not have seen this from the other side if I had not gotten to my birthplace.

Satan did not want me to join this church. He used some people to speak against the leadership of the church, to detour me. They are this and they are that. Yet God saw fit for these particular leaders to become my spiritual family. He set up the connection. And I am confident that it is a true connection because let me tell you something, I have moments when I do not attend church. Some of those moments turned into seasons and because of the connection even when I am not sitting on the pew, I am still spiritually inclined.

So many words that have been taught under the roof of Dominion and Power have laid a durable foundation and structure in my life. It has helped shape and mold me. This is why I can tell my family's story from the inside of the very storm that scattered us. A lot of misjudgment came from outside of the storm.

My mother took a lot of kicks while she was down. I even kicked her myself. I lacked spiritual understanding. I learned from my own understanding. I saw from the outside what Satan wanted me to see. I saw everyone in my way but myself. I desperately longed after the love of others. I waited on people to love me back. I sought acceptance. I looked in all the wrong places. When my place is actually in God, not in this world. I am here on borrowed time. I am here for God's purpose.

Trust me when I tell you the view is not the same. What it looks like from the natural eyes is not what it looks like from the spiritual eyes. Had I not been under a true covering, I would not have learned how to fight back against the attacks. I would not have known that I had the keys to set my loved ones and I free from this bondage.

At one point in our life, a wedge of distance grew between Neka and me. But it did not come from my end. I tried many times to reach out to her, but that created even more distance between us. I prayed about it, and I left it in God's hands. I waited for Him to bring her back to me and He did just that.

I brought my sister into the doors of Dominion and Power and then eventually my whole family attended. This included my mother and all my siblings. It only took that one visit and they have all been back! My mother and Neka started coming on their own with or without me.

Neka's anointing started to take shape. She had given her yes to God. Spiritual understanding brought us even closer together than we were in our childhood. However, she also possessed an internal opposition.

She and I shared the last few years of her life growing closer to God together. She clung to me like a fish on a hook. Neka wanted to be around me all the time. God had brought her closer to me because her time was winding down. At that time, I didn't recognize that God had a plan for our relationship. I just embraced every moment that I had with her and I am thankful that He gave me that moment to do so.

My sister had a gift. She could see the spiritual realm. That is how she was able to see the demon that possessed her in our childhood. She was a prophetic dreamer. Her dreams were not normal. She always dreamed of calamity and destruction. **Back in 2015 Neka's daughter had a vision in the spiritual realm.**

Neka's oldest daughter came to her while she was washing dishes and told her she needed to tell her something. My sister listened to her. My niece told my sister she kept seeing the devil in her brother's room. Neka asked how she knew it was the devil. She began to describe his appearance. This had caught Neka's attention because It was a familiar memory from her own childhood.

So, Neka followed her to the room and asked her if she could still see him and my niece said that she could only see him in the dark. My sister turned off the light and my niece clung on to her mother's leg and said, "There he is mama!" while pointing in Satan's direction. Neka turned the lights back on and instructed her daughter to do exactly what she demonstrated. She started waving her hands and rebuking the devil in Jesus's name.

My niece closely followed her instructions. Neka turned the light off again and my niece held on to her leg tightly and said, **"He's right in front of you and he has a gun and there is blood all over the walls."** Neka said she caught chills, so she turned the lights back on and repeatedly rebuked the devil in Jesus's name. She turned the light back off and my niece said, **"Mom, there goes God. He just walked up to us and put a shield of protection around us. He said we are protected."** She went on describing that the angels were fighting the devil. She saw the devil's chest open up. From it she saw her siblings and Neka's heads being pulled from his chest.

Please, do not sleep on your kids when they are trying to communicate with you. Listen to them instead. My niece did not wake up from a dream telling her mother that. She had a vision while she was awake standing right next to my sister.

Chapter 5

Running Out of Time

God had given me the idea about authoring a book in the beginning of 2017. I started writing but then I got writer's block. Well, what I thought was writer's block was God telling me "No, that is not it." My children and I had stayed the week at Neka's place. She had gotten up around five that morning and she came to me with her right hand raised and said, "Give me a high five! Write that book because it's going to work out for you. God showed me."

Some time had passed. Neka called me one evening and I could hear the fright in her voice. She said, "Tina I was in my closet praying and I asked the Lord to use me to bring my family together. And girl, I felt such a strong presence of sickness and death. I ran out of my closet so fast."

Neka and I always tried to do things to bring our family together. I would cook food and invite everyone over. Sometimes they came and sometimes they were not able to, or they just did not want to. That did not stop me and Neka from coming together and sticking to it. We always came together with each other and our kids. We accompanied one another for the holidays, birthdays, weekends, church services and even for random gatherings. Like I said when God brought her back to me, He brought her closer to me.

She wanted our family to come together and stick together. I encouraged her to do what I did, put it in God's hands for Him to do. I had already put it in His hands.

In the middle of the year, between June and July I was having dreams back-to-back about my sister. I was dreaming of her killing the man that she was dating. This was always one of my biggest fears for Neka. I feared that Neka's anger would cause her to kill someone or to kill herself. I had always prayed against her doing

such things.

When Neka was angry, she was so evil. She took vengeance

into her own hands whenever someone came up against her. When

she picked up a weapon, she did not hesitate to use it. And she was

not hitting below the waist with it either. So, when I was having

these dreams, I was telling her about them. I warned her several

times not to let the enemy cause her to strike out.

I knew that God was showing me this dream about her, but I

did not know that He was showing it to me in reverse. That she

would be the one to be killed. I thought the dream was for me to

give her warning not to give into Satan's deadly plan of destruction.

And truthfully, it could have been just what God intended for me to

do.

The first dream I had was of Neka showing up at my home

beating on the door and asking for my mom. Me and my mom both came to the door, she yelled out, "Tina, I beat him, I just beat him to

death." While she was punching the palm of her hand with her fist.

On top of my dreams, she kept dreaming as well. One of her

dreams was of an old lady standing on the side of a grave and

looking at her. She described the lady with exceptionally long gray,

and white hair. She said she looked like a witch.

Alone with my dreams and her dreams, her oldest daughter

was dreaming as well. My niece told us of her own dream. She had

dreamed that Neka's head was on fire. This dream really bothered

my niece. She was sad when she had told her mom that dream.

On the night of July 29, 2017, it was a Saturday, Neka had

gone out with our twin sisters to celebrate their 25th birthday. Later

in the wee hours of that night, after she had made it home, she was

rushed to the emergency room by ambulance. She was having

episodes which appeared to be seizures. She was sent to the ICU. I

was notified later the following morning. I came into a panic. I went

running around my living room looking for my keys.

God had instructed me to sit down and listen. I sat on my couch and God told me that Neka was going to live, but she was about to experience something before He brought her out and He wanted me to witness it and write about it. He said it is more spiritual than natural.

When I made it to the hospital I was spiritually suited up and armored. As Neka laid in that ICU bed with a tube down her throat and sedated. I stood next to her, and I whispered, "God said you are going to live, but you're going to see some things before He brings you out of this."

She squeezed my hand, and I started praying aloud. I did not care who was standing in the room. I was there with an instructed assignment from God. I was there to be my sister's keeper.

The doctors did not know what was going on with her. They did not understand what was causing the seizure-like episodes. Her alcohol levels were normal. They saw no sign of drugs in her system.

Yet she kept spazzing into these seizure-like episodes. That is how they treated them. They even gave her doses of volume.

Neka stayed in the ICU for 48 hours (about 2 days). The hospital will not allow anyone to stay overnight in the ICU with the patient. They have limited visiting hours. Meanwhile I went to work and came afterwards. One day I was at work, and I was talking with my boss. While she was talking, I heard God. He said, "Go and be with your sister."

I left work and went to be with my sister. That was the day they took her from the ICU and put her in a room. When I walked into the room and my sister laid eyes on me, she was so happy. She said, "There's my sister baby, give me a hug." with her arms wide opened. When I hugged her, she whispered in my right ear and said these words to me, "I love you sister baby and don't let anybody tell you different."

She said loud and clear that if anything happened to her, she wanted me to have her kids and all her belongings. I laughed and I told her I did not want anything that belonged to her because she

was not going anywhere.

She had shared with me about the spiritual encounter she

had while she was in ICU. She said, "Tina when I was in ICU, I saw

the devil coming to get me." She said she was on her way to hell but

our deceased grandmother and Micheal the archangel stood in

front of him and said "Not today devil." She said my grandmother

was dressed in all white. She said they fought for her. She had asked

me to stay the night with her but did not know I had already come

prepared to stay. I had told my boss I would be back to work after I

tended to my sister.

She continued having those seizure-like episodes. We kept

turning her over to her side. We kept time on how long they lasted

and how far they were apart. They were coming back-to-back. My

sister suffered with these episodes for seven days. The doctors were

confused.

They did not understand why the doses of the volume were not working. The more they kept coming, the longer they lasted. And through every episode I was by her side. I was at war with her praying in her ear. Pleading the blood of Jesus over her. Every time she came back to herself, she had something to tell me.

These episodes were draining my sister's strength. Me and my cousins had to bathe her and help her potty. I was sitting on the let-out bed and she was laying there with her eyes closed. She said, there are snakes all over this room floor. I looked down as if I could see what she was saying. She asked me to get in bed with her and I did. Hospital beds are small. So, we were right under each other. Again, she repeated that there were snakes all over the floor of the room. She said I need to get out of here and get to my prayer closet. She said they cannot save me. She asked me if I was scared, and I said "No, I am equipped."

Now if it had not been for God telling me she was going to experience something more spiritual then natural, I would have been scared. The more she shared with me, the more I understood.

My sister was going through tormenting on the other side.

Her body was tensing up tight and shaking every episode.

She made this weird snorkeling noise. She was foaming and spitting

at the mouth. Every time they gave her the medicine through the IV

drip, she screamed intensely from the top of her lungs, "It burns! It

is hot! It is burning me!" She kept requesting ice cold water and to

please turn on the air. We had turned the air down the lowest it

would go. Yet she still screamed it was hot. The room was freezing

cold.

My cousins were there to help. If it was anything to do with a

seizure, they were the ones to know. Their brother suffered from

them. Just as sure as they were there to help, they were there to

witness it too. The doctors had ordered an MRI scan to be done.

They were trying to figure out what those unexplainable seizure-like

episodes were and the cause of them.

The test came back. They told her it was not a seizure, and they did not have a diagnosis for it. They recommended that she's to see a psychiatrist. They gave her a prescription for depression and discharged her that Saturday morning, on August 5, 2017. She had been there since that Sunday morning. She did not accept what they had told her. She knew a psychiatrist could not help and no medicine was strong enough either. This was no matter for medicine.

My little sisters kept our kids. Neka needed some rest and I went with her to her home. Later that evening Neka had another episode. I knew what to do. Her fiancé called for an ambulance once again and they got her. This time we went to another emergency room. My cousin and auntie met us there.

Neka was fighting the nurses who we saw trying to help her. She said they were laughing and picking on her. We were seeing from different sides. Then she calmed down. My auntie leaned over to her and whispered something in her ear. I do not know what it was. My aunt then said aloud, "You know what you gotta do."

The doctors there did not know anything either and discharged her. Again, we went back to her home. That night we lay in bed together and we talked. I watched over her that night as she slept. She smiled in her sleep. That was my sign that she was ok. So, I went to sleep.

The next morning, she told me she saw something standing in the room we slept in before she went to sleep but did not initially say anything to me about it. She said it was big and black, but she was not scared because I was with her. We got up and ate breakfast. She said she wanted to go to church. I was not sure if we should go because I did not want her to have another episode.

However, she said if it were to happen, we would be in the right place. And she was right about it.

We went to church and Apostle Paul called both of us up together and gave us both a word. A word we both needed to hear after the week we had. We were revived. Neka did not have another

seizure-like episode again. We went to my little sister's house. I

cooked and we had a fun time.

There was a revival the following week. It started on August

9, 2007. Neka and I attended every night. We had a guest speaker.

On the last night of revival, the Prophet had prophesied to everyone

in the church. He prophesied to me. He told me I was about to go

through a dry desert but to keep my eye on God and God was going

to see me through.

When he got to Neka, he took her son and held him. My

nephew was being a crybaby. He looked at my sister shaking his

head and said, "You are tired. My sister cried and he embraced her

with a hug.

Me and Neka had discussed a plan to help each other. After

going through what she had just gone through, we agreed to live

our life, becoming what we were set out to do. She had enrolled in

hair school, and I had taken the time off from work to work on my book. I agreed to watch her set of twins while she was in school.

And that is what we were doing. She would drop them off in the

morning and go to school. I was writing a story. I was authoring a

story you will never read because then I was authoring a story that

was not the story God told me to write.

There was a tornado predicted to hit on the weekend. She

had asked me if I was prepared for it. I said yes. Thursday morning,

October 5, 2017, I was up working on my storyline and waiting for

Neka to bring the twins. When she came in the door, she had

thrown a twelve pack of Angel Soft tissue at my head. I did not ask

her to bring me any tissue. This was her own doing. However, I was

down to a few rolls. I said thank you because I need it. She looked at

me with a smirk on her face like, you sure are going to need it. She

left and went to school. She did not stay the entire day.

Around noon time, she showed back up to my apartment to

pick up the twins and her other kids were with her. She got out of

her truck crying. She and her fiancé had exchanged words, and he said some hurtful things to her. They were going through a breakup.

I embraced her with a hug and gave her a few words to encourage

her spirit. She stayed for a little while.

As she was getting ready to go, she did something she had

never done. She kissed my daughter who loves makeup on the lips

and left lipstick on her lips. I was surprised because my sister did not

like to see a child with make up on. She was in better spirits than

when she had shown up.

Later that night around twelve midnight, I was once again on

my computer, staring at its blank screen. I was stuck. The storyline

that I was working on when God said no. I knew it was not the story

He told me to write. He had already given me the story to write. I

just did not want to write it.

I remember hearing two gunshots go off. It was so far away

but loud. I called my neighbor and asked her if she had heard the

two shots fired. She said no and that she was standing outside. Yet I did not know the shots I was hearing were from the spirit realm.

Little did I know her time was winding out.

Chapter 6

Piecing Things Together
(Friday October 6, 2017)

Once again, I was up typing on my computer while waiting for her to bring the twins. She sent a text that stated that she was not coming. I asked why and she replied "Moving". She picked up the phone and called me. We talked about her moving back into her trailer prior to moving in with him. She thanked me for being so encouraging to her. She told me I was such an inspirational and positive person to be around. I asked if she needed me to come and help her move and she said no. She already had her things packed. We ended our phone call with an I love you.

Later that evening around 6pm. I called her to check on her and see how far she had gotten with moving. When she answered she was frustrated because before I could get my question out, she said that she would call me when she got situated.

She never called me back. I called my niece's phone around 8 p.m., I asked her if they had finished moving and she said no. I asked where was her mom and she said in the back arguing. Around 10 p.m. that night, I received a phone call from one of my twin sisters. "Tina, have you talked to Neka? I am hearing she shot her fiancé."

I immediately called Neka's phone and she did not answer. I called my niece's phone and an unfamiliar voice answered. I asked where Neka was. The lady told me she had been shot. I spoke with one of the officers on the scene. He told me she was being airlifted and where to.

It was the other way around. Her fiancé had shot her and then himself all while her children were there. I felt something pulling from me as I fell to my knees in the hallway. I started praying. I was looking for God to speak to me and calm me down like he had done in the past. But He was quiet.

I went to the hospital where she was airlifted. The doctor told us that she had been shot in the head. He said my sister was brain dead and there was nothing they could do but they had encouraged us to pray. I paced the floor. I went into an empty waiting room. I got off in a corner and started praying. Praying for a miracle. A miracle that would leave everyone speechless. I called out to God but again, He did not answer.

All I could hear was the sound of my heart beating, as if it were echoing in an empty hallway. I made an offering to Him. Still, He did not answer. The echoing sound of my heartbeat grew more intense. He was quiet. I walked back to the other waiting room with our family. By the time I could sit down, the doctor came back shaken his head no. Her time was no longer winding. My sister was pronounced dead.

No way! No way! No way! My sister was dead. No, not my sister. Not her. Why her? Show me and I wanted to see her. I wanted to see God perform a miracle to save her. I just needed to touch her, in hopes that she would breathe again. "Wake her up God. Wake her up! What about her kids? What about me?"

And there I was, in that dry desert that had been prophesied to me. She asked me if I were ready for the tornado and I said yes but, I lied. I was not ready for that type of storm. We were expecting it to hit land, and it didn't. At least not in the way we looked for it. However, it did hit, and my sister was swept up in it. In addition to that, I had to be the one to break the news to her kids that she was not coming back.

Remember that sickness and death she felt from her prayer closet? You know, the time when she asked God to use her to bring us together. Well, He used her. We got together when she was in the hospital those seven days. We came together for her death. God prevailed on the enemy's plan.

I was wiping away my tears with the Angel Soft tissue she had thrown at my head; she knew I would need it. The whole time my sister was saying goodbye to me when she was thanking me for being inspirational and positive to her. That kiss she left on my daughter's lips was her farewell kiss. That pulling I felt in my hallway was her letting me go. My fight was letting her go. That was the dryness of the desert.

That dream I had about her showing up to my apartment and beating on my door, yelling, "I just beat him to death!" She was really telling me she beat Satan's plans against her. He could not drag her soul to hell by suicide. He could not trap her in cell by committing a homicide from that demon he possessed in her that filled her with all that vengeful anger. He could not take her soul.

My niece had that vision two years prior to her mother's death. She saw God's angels fight for their family. She saw them win. She saw Satan lose that battle. She saw their souls coming out of Satan's chest. That is why I said He could not take her soul. God would not allow it. It was already won before it ever occurred in the natural realm.

Neka understood something that I did not. God showed Neka that hell is real during those seven days in the hospital. When she got out of that hospital, she came out determined to get her life right. Life is too precious to waste it. Hair was always her thing. She could braid your hair into a bouquet of flowers if that is what you wanted. She enrolled in hair school and was loving every second of it. I am glad she spent her last days doing what she loved.

I still believe that until this day, Neka knew she did not have a lot of time left. She had all her things packed and set up to move in the natural realm. In fact, she did move. She transitioned over into the heavenly realm instead.

***The images of the text messages show some of the final conversations between both Neka and I. The last few pictures displays her packed household items. I believe that Neka knew that her time was running out soon. These messages took place from September 6th – October 6th (her final day here on earth). Take a look.

We need to get prepared for da storm.
Call aunt Dessi
When is it coming
Why
I guess da weekend they don't know which way.. but it's a lot of ppl gettin prepared buying out water and everything dats y I asked u if u had stamps.
Tlk to everyone about having a dinner
Oh ok
I'll call her tomorrow
Ok
S= Sister and M= Me

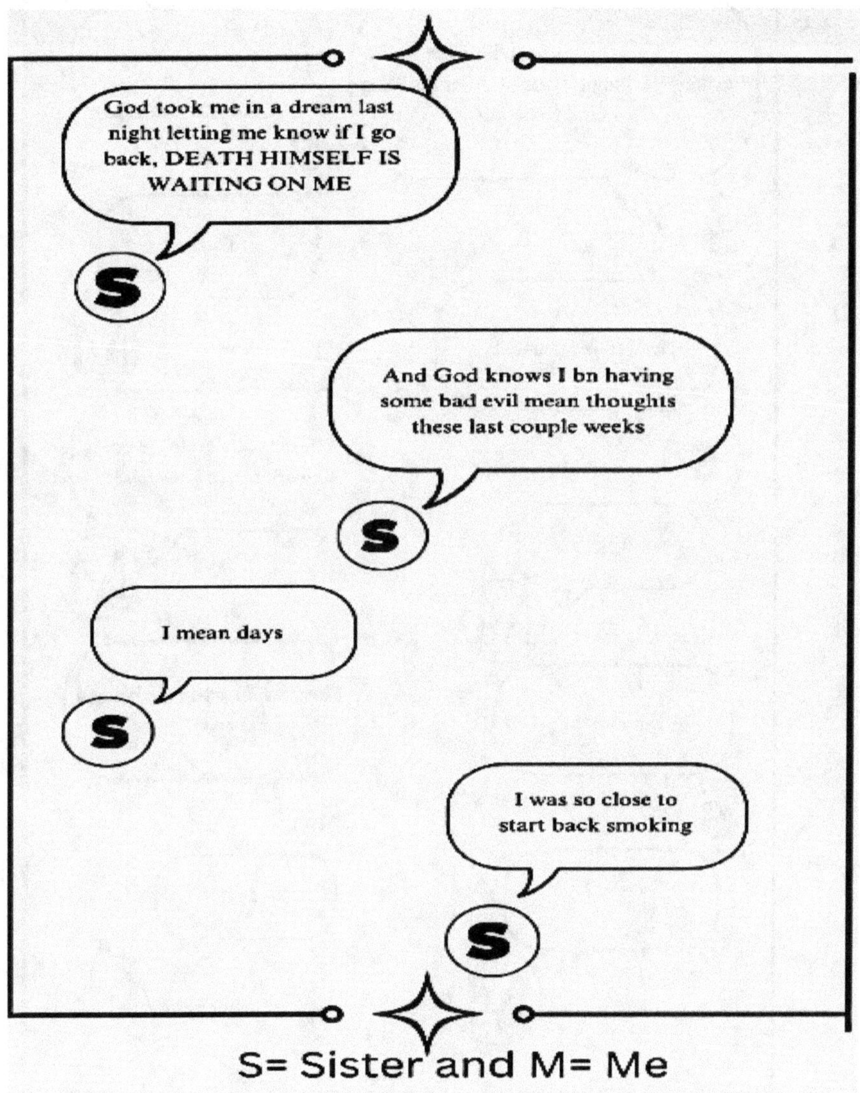
God took me in a dream last night letting me know if I go back, DEATH HIMSELF IS WAITING ON ME
And God knows I bn having some bad evil mean thoughts these last couple weeks
I mean days
I was so close to start back smoking
S= Sister and M= Me

S= Sister and M= Me

Upon retrieving Neka's belongings from her new trailer, I stumbled upon a striking image adorning the refrigerator: angelic wings sketched delicately, yet no one knew how it got there or the artist. Despite my sister's belongings still being packed away, this mysterious drawing stood proudly on display, its significance remains concealed in suspense till this very day.

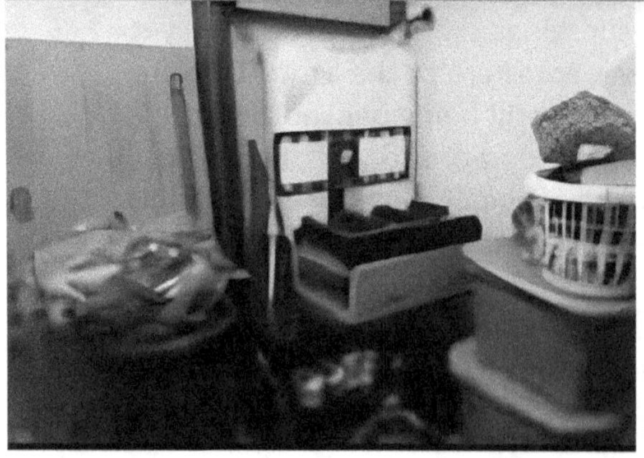

Chapter 7

Through The Dry Desert

Here's a definition for you. **Through** - moving in one side and out of the other side of; continuing in the time toward completion of a process period.

I have had to endure a lot of things, but this was the process that gracefully broke me down. I did not know the strength of my endurance until it was challenged. Seeing my sister lay in that casket was rough, but it was the going through part that was rougher. It was dry and painful.

I threw some nasty tantrums, I shut off from the world and I would not open the door to anybody. I didn't even want my kids around me, nor could I eat or sleep. I had lost weight and most of all, I had lost my girl. Hate was starting to consume me. That pain had inflicted all the other old wombs. I had become so resentful and angry with God and men. I was depressed and sitting in the dark.

Every time I saw other sisters out together, sorrow set in, and tears welled up in my chest. I was an emotional wreck. I was isolated. I kept asking God why. Why did this have to be my life, my story. Why did that man take my sister from her kids? Why did he take her from me? What he prophesied about that desert was right.

It was indeed dry, but I had to go through it. I was like Jonah in the Bible. Mad and angry while running away from the assignment. I was running away from my own story. The very story He had given me to write about. My family's story.

When I wrote it the first time, I thought that I was done. God said no and I felt discouraged, so I left it alone. As much as I like to write, a book was out of my league. Then He instructed me to author my story again. I wrote it a second time. God said not quite. I left it alone again. God said author the story. I wrote a third time. The third time is a charm, right? God said write it again. I said God this is too much pressure. You told me to author my story and I did. Why do I keep having to write it over? I left it alone again. Each time I began to grow lazier and lazier. I lost my desire to write.

God had put me in an isolation season. He said do not be disturbed. He isolated me from everybody, but my kids and they did not even bother me. For seven weeks I was isolated. He was my only source. I had nothing but time, so I prayed without ceasing. I studied His words and I fasted. God said author the book. Every other time He said, author the story. This time He said author the book.

I was rough drafting and reading all the other stories I had written. While doing so God showed me the difference in each one.

The first time I drafted my story it was from a place of resentment and anger. That is all you would have gotten from it. The second time, I was the accuser. The third time the healing was starting to show. I was not only seeing the transition on paper, but I was becoming the transition while so. He said, **"This is why I kept making you write it over. I was making you over."**

He allowed me to write it repeatedly and each one was the becoming of my healing. The pressure was necessary. I got beat with the ugly end of the stick, but my scars healed beautifully. The process broke me gracefully. God had to break down what that seed of discord created inside of me. It did not feel good and It was painful. However, I found out that there is beauty in the broken. Believe that!

When God tells you to do something, do it. You may think that flaw about you cannot be used, but God's hands can and will create the most magnificent masterpiece. You may have an ugly story, but you will be one beautiful sculpture if you allow God to make you over. You can try and fix what is broken with your two hands, but all it takes is one of God's hands. You do not know what is attached to your assignment, or better yet who is attached to your assignment.

Can you hear the calling on your life? The farther you run, the louder the calling gets. Myself for example, there was a time ago when I clubbed. One night I was at the club in the bathroom and this girl told me I looked like a First Lady. I will not lie; I was offended because I was never half stepping when I went out clubbing. I was half naked and didn't have on any church shoes. In fact, I wore stilettos without a church hat on. So how did I look like a First Lady? And who would think of saying that in a club? I had on a piece of a dress (more like a piece of fabric).

The point is, if you hear the calling on your life, answer it. You are not escaping it because you do not answer it. However, you will be left behind if you do not answer it, because you do not know who or how many souls are attached to your calling. I know that I do not want anybody's blood on my hands. I hope you do not either. If you are a runner, stop running.

What is the calling? The answer is your purpose. Your purpose operates under the authority of the spirit not your fleshly desires. Do not worry about who is not going to accept you. Keep in mind, "For God I live, for God I die." You are not living for acceptance, just do your part. Either they accept you or not, as you will not be held accountable if they choose not to take heed.

The hardest part about being chosen for a purpose is having to go through something that connects you to your purpose. Your purpose requires going through hell. If it sounds better, your purpose requires suffering. Before Saul became Paul, he was a pharisee who intensely persecuted the followers of Jesus. However, God had chosen Saul to be His vessel. What did God say to Ananias about Saul? Jesus said He would show him how many things he must suffer for His name's sake.

"Then Ananias answered, "Lord I have heard from many about this man, how much harm he has done to Your saints in Jerusalem. And here he has authority from the chief priests to bind all who call on Your name." But the Lord said to him, "Go, for he is a chosen vessel of Mine to bear My name before Gentiles, kings, and the children of Israel.
For I will show him how many things he must suffer for My name's sake" (Acts 9:13-16 NKJV).

Therefore, when you are chosen you will suffer for the sake of God's name. I would rather suffer for God than to suffer for nothing. It would be unfortunate to go through all that hell and it is not for the sake of God. Why? Because if it is not for God, it is for nothing, it is in vain. The thing about going through hell for God is, He makes you fireproof. You will come out without a burn.

My mother had the perfect family to go through that storm. She equipped us with the word and with prayer. It never left us. Neither of us departed from that path in which she trained us up in. If she had known that God had chosen her family to suffer for His name's sake and to save and set free families, she would have given hers up freely without the storm.

Especially with the heart she served God with when I was a little girl. Like the story of Abraham. That man was ready to kill his own son for God's sake. Has someone ever spoken a word to you saying, God is going to use you to save your family, or someone? What do you think about when He says use you? The requirements of being used by God may cause you to have to lose something or someone to save something or someone. **Will you say yes?**

Chapter 8

Why Not Me?

The positive and inspirational traits about me that drew my sister closer to my likeness was nothing but God's light shining straight through me! My sister felt the love of God through me. In the book of Matthews when Jesus was teaching the crowd one of the people from the crowd asked, **"…Good Teacher, what good thing shall I do so that I may have eternal life?"** And Jesus answered, **"Why do you call Me good? No one is good but One, that is, God. But if you want to enter life, keep the commandments" (Matthew 19:16-17 NKJV).**

Therefore, if I had not had the love of God in me, she would not have seen the good in me. All glory be to God. I take none of the credit for this. We can do no good thing without God. Read it for yourself.

When I do not understand something, I have this weird habit of drawing or writing the problem out on paper and then I make sense of it. I am weird to some and slow to others, but it works for me. I must have picked the habit up during the times my mind was under attack and my imagination was no longer my safe place.

I have this thing where I can see the good inside of the bad. Call it optimistic, but I call it a gift from God. In the book of James, he tells the people to consider their troubles as an opportunity to grow their endurance. I guess that's why God chose me for the job. God knew who I was before my time. He knew who I was when I was sitting at that window waiting for two of His angels to descend from the sky and fly me to heaven to be with Him. When I learned who I was in Christ, I learned my strength. I learned that I had willpower when I started walking in His will. I am who God says I am.

Satan tried to strip me from my identity. He did not want me to know who I was in Christ Jesus. He started stripping me in my childhood. I endured the bullying and the molestation, but he played me at my weakness. I desperately wanted a bond with my mom and my dad. And because I did not have it, I felt alone and left behind. I felt overlooked. I felt all the issues of abandonment. "I FELT." What I felt was all falsified. Why do we move off a feeling? LOVE is not to be felt, it is to be shown. It is not a feeling but an action. I used to be so caught up in the world's perception of love that it caused me to look like a big fool and hurt some people. I was a fool talking about how I do not feel loved to the very ones who did love me. Not only was I a fool, but I was doing foolish things. I was a fool looking for a feeling. Just dumb. I wanted to be loved when in fact I was, but I was too blinded by a falsified feeling that I did not see love loving me or taking care of me. I thought being loved meant being liked. I thought being loved meant communication. I thought being loved was something I was supposed to feel. So, I was out there seeking something that did not exist in those means. I was looking in some places that were meant to destroy me. I was deceived. Tricked into thinking it was love I was looking for when the whole time it was entrapment to keep me trapped. The more I looked from here to there, the more I was trapped within a maze. I was losing my power to the enemy. Satan knew who and what to send my way to keep me trapped. Every time I thought I was coming out; I was walking into another trap. My entire soul was trapped.

I had to leave my soul trapped and find the way out. I had to leave me behind. All the while, I was caught up in some places that detoured me. That caused stagnation, delay and setbacks.

I met my good friend, the minister. God put me in my birthing place. Had He not, I would not have known my healing was attached to my anointing. If my anointing cannot heal me, it could not heal anyone else. I had to be the first.

Once upon a time I thought I was too damaged to be loved. Then I stopped seeking after human love and love started shaping me. God is love. Satan tried to kill my purpose using my hands. I said it once and I'll say it again. He played me against me. He knows my purpose has good usage. Usage to save a wretch like thee. And my God prevailed on top of his plans.

"…When the enemy comes in like a flood, The Spirit of the LORD will lift a standard against him" (Isaiah 59:19).

If God allowed it, He has a plan to prevail on it. He gave Satan permission to go after Job, just to show us **He will prevail**. Forgive that man that violated you. Forgive your parents who left you. Forgive yourself for sleeping on you. Forgive period. Everyone deserves it. If you do not forgive them, that does not stop God from forgiving them. That is, you are putting a hindrance on yourself. Do not be so focused on being the accuser. Among several other names, Satan is known as the accuser.

You do not want to be the one to bust hell wide open for a grudge, when the one you blame for the grudge makes it into the gates of heaven. Do not let Satan deceive you out of your soul's salvation. If you do not forgive, you will be left behind. Forgive and heal. Be cautious of that feeling. It will lead you to a place you may not come back from. And if you do, check yourself, because you may have come out with something else attached to you. Another attachment is another problem.

You see, the very thing that had attached itself to my soul was the very thing that had to be disarmed. The only reason I am testifying is because of the truth. The truth set me free. Once upon a time I did not know the truth because everything I thought I knew was falsified. I knew a fabricated truth. Satan does not want you to know the truth because he knows the truth shall set you free. He does not want you free, he wants you dumb and captive. He will strip you of what you know and give you what he wants you to know. He will play off your fleshly desires. So, discipline that flesh. Get it under submission or else be controlled. Give him no ammunition. Give him no power over your life. Confess your sins. Do not hide in them because all you are doing is making a trap for yourself. Your soul will never be at rest in this matter. You will make a mess of your life. Ask God to search your soul and to bring anything out that is hidden. The soul is trapped in a very dark place, so ask God to shine His light within and to strengthen you. I am telling you now that it must be God's light. Other "lights" will miss it, but God's light will dismiss it. Do not go to everybody but God. You must open up and talk to them only for them to diagnose you with their belief, but you do not have to do anything but look to God. He knows your story. When He shows it to you, do not close your eyes. See it and deal with it. Do not try to walk your healing journey alone. Invite God to go before you, with you and to be the defender behind you.

"And ye shall know the truth, and the truth shall make you free" (John 8:32).

I used to dream this same dream from my childhood up until the beginning of my adulthood. I would dream of me standing in front of a big mansion that had similar features to a castle. Outside of the castle were these golden lion statues. There were two, one on each side of the entrance, with a few steps. I walked up the steps and went into the mansion. It was decorated with big and heavy beautiful gold decorations, but it was not cluttered with decorations.

There were thick and heavy drapes with curtains on the windows, but it was light shining through them. I could feel a presence, but I never saw anybody. It was always just me walking around and admiring the beauty of it all. However, there was the sound of musical instruments playing. I dreamed this same dream for a long time.

I knew it was a reason I was having this same dream, but I did not know why. It was not until a few years ago, I was sitting by myself and elaborating on the dream to God. I was in a place in life when I was trying to find my purpose. God spoke to me and told me why I kept having those continuous dreams. He said to me, **"Daughter, I have called you to a place to do my will. You will help build my Kingdom."**

Why not me? When I learned my identity in Christ, I learned that I was the woman fit for the job. I am her. I am a lioness. I am connected to His will. **I am becoming.**

Acknowledgements

Thank God for loving me and entrusting me to write my family's story. It is an honor to do His kingdom's work. To my mother, you were my First Lady before any First Lady. Thank you for training me in the way I should go. You kept me grounded in who I was becoming. You have strong determination and because of it you too, are becoming. I love you lady.

I thank God for connecting me to my spiritual family and birthplace. To Psalmist Keisha Brown Cooley, the start of my connection. You were my first friend to walk in the opposite direction of the world. You are a phenomenal woman of God. I love you sis.

To the founders of Dominion and Power and my overseers Dr. Apostle Paul Beard and Dr. Elect Lady Donna Beard, thank you for your work in the kingdom. Because of your work, I can build on a solid foundation. I am glad to be connected to your ministry. I love you both.

To The Young Apostle Cordaryl Beard and The Ambitious Elect Lady Jessica Beard, thank you for your ambitious and continuous work. Apostle Cordaryl, you inspired the very title of my book. You preached a message on October 1st 2023, entitled "I Am

Becoming". It was extremely relatable to me, and it blessed me dearly. My heart will forever be filled with that message. Elect Lady Jessica I love your enthusiasm for God and the church. You are gracefully unapologetic in what you do, and I admire that.

To my family and friends who kept me encouraged, thank you and I love you. It is true that it takes a village to raise a child. Especially a child of God.

To my dear friend Keisha Kay Cole Robinson, thank you so much for your support. You held my hands through this process. I love you, my girl.

I would also like to give a huge thank you to Mrs. Teaira Curry (Coach Tea) with "Changed Up Now What LLC". A company that helps others to birth out their goals in business and in their personal relationships. I appreciate you for helping me to finally publish my book. As stressful as writing a book can be, you stayed patient with me and walked me through each part with baby steps. You were very kind and encouraging along the way. I pray for continued growth and prosperity regarding your business.

I could not forget about the other contributors of this book. Dennis Expose thank you so much for your time and dedication towards the graphic designs for this book. You came in promptly and brought my vision into a tangible reality.

Chris Maul, I appreciate you for taking the photos for my book cover! Along with all of the time and efforts you put into listening to my story and being led by God to assist me.

To my brother, my mother's only son. Thank you for every moment that you made me laugh tears from out of my eyes. You were the life of any event. You lived out your purpose. I miss you as well.

Last but definitely not least. To my loving sister, Neka. I will miss you dearly. Here is a special thank you. You were right, my book worked for me. I miss you so much!

www.ingramcontent.com/pod-product-compliance
Lightning Source LLC
Chambersburg PA
CBHW050547160726
48003CB00002B/790

9 798869 385611